TRANSPARENCY

30 DEVOTIONS TO ENCOURAGE AND EMPOWER YOUNG WOMEN IN THEIR WALK WITH CHRIST

Kylie Junkin

WESTBOW
PRESS®
A DIVISION OF THOMAS NELSON
& ZONDERVAN

WestBow Press books may be ordered through booksellers or by contacting:

WestBow Press
A Division of Thomas Nelson & Zondervan
1663 Liberty Drive
Bloomington, IN 47403
www.westbowpress.com
844-714-3454

Because of the dynamic nature of the Internet, any web addresses or links contained in this book may have changed since publication and may no longer be valid. The views expressed in this work are solely those of the author and do not necessarily reflect the views of the publisher, and the publisher hereby disclaims any responsibility for them.

Any people depicted in stock imagery provided by Getty Images are models, and such images are being used for illustrative purposes only.
Certain stock imagery © Getty Images.

Scripture marked (NKJV) taken from the New King James Version®. Copyright © 1982 by Thomas Nelson. Used by permission. All rights reserved.

Scripture quotations marked (NIV) are taken from the Holy Bible, New International Version®, NIV®. Copyright © 1973, 1978, 1984, 2011 by Biblica, Inc.® Used by permission of Zondervan. All rights reserved worldwide. www.zondervan.com The "NIV" and "New International Version" are trademarks registered in the United States Patent and Trademark Office by Biblica, Inc.®

Scripture quotations marked (NLT) are taken from the Holy Bible, New Living Translation, copyright ©1996, 2004, 2015 by Tyndale House Foundation. Used by permission of Tyndale House Publishers, Carol Stream, Illinois 60188. All rights reserved.

Scripture quotations marked CSB have been taken from the Christian Standard Bible®, Copyright © 2017 by Holman Bible Publishers. Used by permission. Christian Standard Bible® and CSB® are federally registered trademarks of Holman Bible Publishers.

Scripture quotations marked HCSB are taken from the Holman Christian Standard Bible®, Used by Permission HCSB ©1999,2000,2002,2003,2009 Holman Bible Publishers. Holman Christian Standard Bible®, Holman CSB®, and HCSB® are federally registered trademarks of Holman Bible Publishers.

ISBN: 978-1-6642-7355-9 (sc)
ISBN: 978-1-6642-7356-6 (hc)
ISBN: 978-1-6642-7354-2 (e)

Library of Congress Control Number: 2022913787

Print information available on the last page.

WestBow Press rev. date: 07/28/2022

This book is dedicated to my little sister Hannah.
May your love for Jesus grow stronger
with every breath you take.

CONTENTS

PREFACE

Let's be real. Life is hard.

Even if you are like me and grew up in a caring family who loves Jesus, that does not mean you aren't going to struggle. It doesn't provide exemption from harsh words, body shame, self-image issues, loss, grief, or failure. You name it—we have all experienced it in some form or fashion.

While following Jesus is the greatest decision anyone could ever make, that doesn't mean it's easy. If your brain works like mine, reading the scriptures that promise we will be persecuted just like Jesus was can kind of hurt my feelings sometimes. When I am really going through it, it's honestly difficult for me to find comfort in that.

Here's the beautiful thing though: Jesus was completely human, just like you and me. That means that He has felt every single negative feeling that we experience in our lives. In addition, He was completely God, which means He knows how to teach us the way to live righteously. We serve a God who understands and loves in a way that is beyond belief, and it blows my mind every day. And that is the reason I wrote this devotional. I want teen girls and young women everywhere to be bold in their faith instead of feeling guilty that they are upset because "Christians are supposed to be happy." I want you to be stronger than I was. I want you to see yourself the way God does. I will gladly be the one to struggle so you can walk a little easier in your faith.

So, buckle up. Get ready to get real. Get vulnerable. Get stronger. Get bolder. I have already prayed over you as you walk through this journey. I am not perfect by any means, but I pray that you find comfort in knowing you are not alone in your struggles. I hope you never forget that God does his best work with broken things.

Girl you are so loved,
Kylie Junkin

1

IT SHOULDN'T BE ABOUT ME

$$\gg$$

And he said to him, "Son, you are always with me, and all that I have is yours. It was right that we should make merry and be glad, for your brother was dead and is alive again, and was lost and is found."

—LUKE 15:31–32 (NKJV)

$$\ll$$

I've never considered myself a selfish or self-centered person. I hate being in the spotlight, so I thought I was "good" in that area. Well, when you ask God to make you into the person He wants you to be, He does just that. And let me tell you, it hurts! But in the end, it is oh so worth it.

We all go through life desperately wanting someone to notice and support us. We work hard. We stress out. While we may not want our names on a billboard, we still want to have some kind of praise for the effort we've put in. I've been broad, but please bear with me as I get real. When we're real, it can be really ugly.

My church hired a new youth minister my senior year of high school. He and his wife were both amazing and I loved what they had done for the church. The problem though was this: they didn't treat me the way my last youth minister and his wife did. I mean, I was the favorite, the go-to, and the best friend. But now, with these new people, I was just another "leader," just like everyone else in the youth group.

Truth be told, I was angry about it. So what did I do? I did what has the most power—I prayed. Understand that it can be dangerous, asking God to reveal why you feel the way you do. It can kick you in the gut really quick. Do you want to know the response I got? God said, "Kylie, it's not all about you." Whoa. Talk about a knife through the heart; am I right?

As I began to let that harsh reality sink in, I began to see all the good things about those people that I had overlooked in my anger. God had brought them all the way from Texas to be our ministers—not *mine* but *ours*. This kind of conviction applies to every area of life.

There will be times where we work our hind ends off and don't even get a thank you. Is it easy? No. Do we get angry? Yes, but we must remember that, when we're doing the will of God, it is never about us. It's always about the God who made us. Living that out, daily, gets us more than a mere "thank you" from our peers. It gets us a "well done" from God Himself.

How can you put others first today?

2

GOD IS ENOUGH

≫

I am the bread of life. He who comes to me shall never hunger, and he who believes in me shall never thirst.

—JOHN 6:35 (NKJV)

≪

We can all agree that life is not easy, at all. There are times where it feels like we're being hit from every side. Trust me, I know. I've seen my fair share of broken homes, lives, and hearts. Honestly, in about 98 percent of those times, I've called God's goodness into question. "Why is this happening to me? I thought God wanted me to be happy. Bad things happening to me means God doesn't love me, right?" *No!* That's where I was wrong.

Looking back, if I had to do it all over again, I wouldn't change a single "bad" thing that I've been through. But please, don't misunderstand me. I'm not saying this because my life is perfect right now. I'm writing this with a broken heart, having no idea where to go, and not having a clue if I'm going to get where I want to be. You may be thinking, "Kylie, how in the world can you say you wouldn't change that you've been hurt and are hurting right now?"

My answer is this: you are right; there is no way *in this world* that I can say that. My hope lies in Jesus, who has overcome the world. He has shown up and redeemed every ounce of pain I've ever experienced. He is constantly holding me, guiding me, and loving me. Is it easy? Not always. Let's be real. It's hard! I don't like not knowing and having to wait. The only thing that keeps me going is that I serve a living God, who would literally move the universe for me. He is that powerful!

Do I want to feel as loved by my earthly father as I love him? Yes. However, God has used that pain to show me the unconditional love of my heavenly Father. Do I want back all those old friends who abandoned me? Yes, but God used that loneliness to show me true Christian fellowship.

Do I have moments where I think I want ex-boyfriends back? Yes. However, God is using those hurts to remind me to be patient and trust His timing because He knows best. There will always be an excuse not to sell out to God. When you ask God to show up in your life, He will show you all the reasons why following Him is the only way to be restored.

God truly is all we need. When we give our all to Him, all that hurt will begin to heal and everything else will fall into place.

Please never forget this: God knows every moment of our lives and loves us as if He didn't.

What is one hurt that you can lay at the feet of Jesus today?

3
WORDS

⩔

Let no corrupt word proceed out of your mouth,
but what is good for necessary edification,
that it may impart grace to the hearers.

—EPHESIANS 4:29 (NKJV)

⩓

Okay, I know this verse is thrown around a lot, but I don't think people really let it sink in. Most people use this verse as an excuse not to cuss. While that is a part of the meaning of "corrupt" words, that is not all it means. "You're ugly. Why do you dress like that? You look dumb. Did you hear what she did?" Any of those sound familiar? Sure they do.

We've all heard and used them a million times. We must remember that every single person on the planet is loved and made in the image of God. That means that our words should be drenched in love, kindness, encouragement, and honesty.

So let's use God's filter and change those statements. "You're beautiful. Your style is so unique! You look incredible. Did you hear that she got saved?" You never know what someone is going through. Most of the time, reality is a whole lot different from what people try to portray. You've done it; I've done it. We pretend everything is okay when we feel like we're dying inside. So choose your words carefully because, if we're being honest, we still remember those words that people said to us, so long ago.

Look, I know this is cliché, but words are your witness. If what comes out of your mouth isn't loving, then we aren't imitating Jesus now, are we?

―――――――――――

Who can you speak kindness over today?

4

HEARTBREAK

*And we know that, in all things, God works
for the good of those who love him, who have
been called according to his purpose.*

—ROMANS 8:28 (NIV)

I'm going to be really honest with you. While writing this, I am, straight up, not having a good time. I've been in pain for months over a breakup. I've experienced both highs and lows during that time. We still had friendly conversations, but he also said and did some things that hurt, this week especially. Let me be real; I did a very difficult thing.

I told him I deserved better than what I was getting, and I needed to step back until he could figure out what he wanted. It is so hard because I've prayed for him every day, for nearly two years now. I still love him, despite the pain he's caused me. I'm confused because I was certain God told me things would be different. That honestly hurts, in the depths of my soul.

Do I understand why God is telling me one thing while people act another? No. Do I understand why I still love him more today than I did yesterday? No. Do I understand why my heart must be broken like this? No. Do I trust that God has a plan? Absolutely, I do. I'm not going to lie and say heartbreak gets easier after a few months because it hasn't for me, yet.

Let me tell you what I do know and understand. Some things must be torn down before they can be rebuilt. God has a purpose for my pain. We are prizes to our Lord Jesus, and anyone who treats us differently is not worth our time.

I wake up every morning and tell myself, "I don't

understand, but I trust God." Trusting God can be difficult, when the process is so slow and painful. We just have to remember that everything will fall into place the way it is supposed to. And it will be better than we could have ever imagined, in the end.

Stay strong, trust God, and be patient.

Reflect on some past hurts that God has redeemed. With those in mind, how can you better trust His plan in the future?

5

FRIENDS

*He who walks with wise men will be wise, but
the companion of fools will be destroyed.*

—PROVERBS 13:20 (NKJV)

It is easy to think that your preschool friends will be there for you, forever. Well, I hate to burst your bubble, but they most likely won't be. I'll be the first to admit that losing friends is worse than losing boyfriends. There are times when we feel so alone and unwanted. In those moments and, really, all the time, I encourage you to pray for godly friends to come into your life.

You don't need a ton of friends because, trust me, having just one or two who will hold you accountable and point you to Jesus is so refreshing. It's about quality over quantity. God may allow you to lose people, but He will never let you be alone. We were made for godly fellowship.

And remember, just because people claim to be Christ followers, doesn't mean they are. If the people you are hanging around aren't pointing you towards Jesus, then there's a problem. It's never easy having to walk away from the people you thought were always going to be there for you, but ultimately you will save yourself a lot of heartache if you do. Seek out those people whose words and actions line up with scripture and be one of those people yourself. In the words of my beloved former youth pastor, Carson Windle, you are who you hang out with.

Are your current friends pushing you closer to Jesus or pulling you farther away?

6

LETTING GO

*To everything there is a season, and a
time to every purpose under heaven.*

—ECCLESIASTES 3:1 (NKJV)

Nothing that is worth it is ever easy.

Let me say that again. The best things in life are not easy to obtain, but man are they worth it. You may be thinking, "Kylie, I've heard this before." Well, let me ask you this. Would you rather have stress free or rewarding? You can't always have both.

Moving on is never easy, especially when it means letting go of someone you care about so deeply. In those moments when we know God is telling us to let go, we tend to plead and beg God to change His mind. I know I have. Now please hear me when I say that is totally okay. It's okay to ask God why sometimes. However, understand that He may not always give you the answer. God has so much more in store for you than you could ever imagine. When He asks you to let go of something good, He is going to replace it with something great. Realize that it may not happen immediately, but God only wants what is best for you. He loves you too much to let you settle for "good." He promises you greatness beyond your wildest dreams. So yes, letting go is difficult, but when we decide to stop just going through hard times and start growing through them, that's when joy comes, when peace settles, and blessings flow. Just trust and hang on.

What is one thing God has been calling you to let go of?

7

WHAT YOU'RE WORTH

So, the King will greatly desire your beauty;
Because He is your Lord, worship Him.

—PSALM 45:11 (NKJV)

As women, we constantly struggle with how we see ourselves. I know I have, and I know you have too. We tend to let the opinions of others and our own past mistakes dictate our worth.

Fortunately, that just isn't true.

You're worth more than the grade on your test. You're worth more than the numbers on the scale. You're worth more than the amount of likes on Instagram. You're worth more than the words said behind your back. You're worth more than the made-up reasons those "friends" used to walk away. You're worth more than your Snap score. You're worth more than what that hormonal boy tried to take from you. You are worth more than the amount of free time your schedule allows. You're worth more than that parent telling you he or she didn't love you or that you weren't good enough. Please hear me when I tell you, *you are worth it*. You're worth it. You're worth love and mercy and grace. You're worth the blood shed on Calvary of a spotless, precious Savior. You are loved far more than your brain can fathom. Honey, you are enough. God is constantly trying to tell you that. Why are you letting other people convince you of anything different?

What is one thing that you like about yourself?

8

DON'T BE AFRAID
TO SPEAK UP

"Moreover, if your brother sins against you, go and tell him his fault between you and him alone. If he hears you, you have gained your brother."

—MATTHEW 18:15 (NKJV)

It is a known fact that I hate conflict. I do not like to confront people. I do not like the feeling of people being mad at me. It makes me cry just thinking about it, to be quite honest.

If we sit in a corner with our feelings all bottled up inside, then we are tempted. Tempted to hold grudges. Tempted to hate and be angry. Tempted to commit murder in our hearts. I know that is intense, but it is true. You know it is.

As the Bible says, we must speak up. We must be uncomfortable. Now, I'm not saying go yell and scream and cast blame. That never works. But if someone has sinned against you or is hindering your spiritual growth, intentionally or not, you need to tell that person. Tell that person out of love and with a gentle spirit. That makes the person more inclined to listen, respect you, and hopefully change for the better.

As you know, though, not everything works out so smoothly. There will be people who act like children and throw a tantrum no matter how gently and lovingly you approach a topic. In those situations, you just must walk away, pray for them, and continue being kind. Doing those things doesn't always make them apologize, but I promise you'll have more peace in your heart knowing you did what Jesus told you to do.

Who do you need to have a tough conversation with this week?

9

HIS STRENGTH, NOT YOURS

*Not by might nor by power, but by My
Spirit, says the LORD of hosts.*

—ZECHARIAH 4:6 (NKJV)

I would never have picked a verse from a lesser known book of the Old Testament had God not prompted me to do so this morning. Yes, the Old Testament is filled with seemingly harsh judgments and wrath, but if you pay attention, some of the most amazing movements of God occur there as well.

In this passage of scripture, the prophet Zechariah describes one of his God-given visions. Now, sometimes all those metaphors and parables confuse me, but through prayer and studying, I truly believe what God is trying to tell us in that passage is the best things happen when we stop trying to take control.

I know that is very difficult for most of us. I especially love to be able to plan and control what's happening to me. However, I can honestly say that some of my most eye-opening growth moments happened when I just let go. Let's take my life situation right now for example. I fought God after my last high-school boyfriend broke up with me. I begged and pleaded that He would change His mind. I wasn't angry with God. I still prayed for His will, but I was upset and felt like He was being silent, nonetheless. After many, many breakdowns, I heard a song and started playing it on my speaker in my room. Instantly I hit the floor. I physically could not stand up. I could only rest on my knees and cry uncontrollably. I felt God so closely in that moment. And I felt that whisper in my heart from Him. The gist of what I heard was this: "Kylie I know you love him, but you need to trust Me. Let me drive for a while and I'll show you how great things can be. Will you be patient and just trust Me?"

I still get chills talking about this encounter. Here is what I want you to take from this: stop trying to do it all yourself and let God carry you. Life is much more blessed when you do.

What is one area of your life that you can give God control over?

10

JESUS ON EVERY PAGE

"Judah, you are he whom your brothers shall praise; your hand shall be on the neck of your enemies; your father's children shall bow down before you. Judah is a lion's whelp; from the prey, my son, you have gone up. He bows down, he lies down as a lion; and as a lion who shall rouse him? The scepter shall not depart from Judah, nor a lawgiver from between his feet, until Shiloh comes; and to Him shall be the obedience of the people. Binding his donkey to the vine, and his donkey's colt to the choice vine, he washed his garments in wine, and his clothes in the blood of grapes. His eyes are darker than wine, and his teeth whiter than milk."

—GENESIS 49:8–12 (NKJV)

Okay, I know you are probably thinking that these are some random Old Testament verses, but before you dismiss it, I want you to think of everything you know about Jesus. Then reread these verses with that in mind. Go ahead, I'll wait …

I am writing this on the very last day of 2019, and as I'm reading, all my thoughts shift to everything that's happened this year. It's been a lot for me physically, mentally, and especially emotionally. I spent the first six months in a relationship, and I have spent the last six months "dating Jesus" and working on myself. There has been plenty of heartache, love, and loss, but there's also been eye-opening revelations and growth.

After reading that paragraph, you are probably wondering how in the world my year has anything to do with the verses from Genesis. Well, here's the answer: our stories were written a long time ago. The details may seem insignificant, but if we ask God, He'll show us all the places where Jesus showed up.

Here's the background. Judah was one of Jacob's (a.k.a. Israel) twelve sons. They are often referred to as the twelve tribes of Israel. Jacob's grandfather was Abraham, whom God promised to make the father of many nations. Looking ahead at the New Testament, in the very first chapter of Matthew is the genealogy of Jesus Christ. Here is where it starts to come together. The first four people that Jesus descended from are none other than Abraham, Isaac, Jacob, and—you guessed it—Judah.

"Okay Kylie, thanks for the history lesson, but how do I apply this to my life?" The answer is a Sunday school one: Jesus. These verses foreshadow Jesus's strength, His power, His kingship, and how He came to fulfill the law without question. It hints at His water to wine miracle, riding on a donkey on Palm Sunday, the comparison between Him and the vine, and even the shedding of His blood.

How amazing is that, right? Jesus is everywhere, and He desperately wants to be in a committed, loving relationship with us. He's constantly pursuing you. Think about it. The Creator of the universe and Almighty King of Kings wants you, just as you are, and just as He made you. He wants to show you the miraculous things that can happen if you love Him. This is probably all stuff you already know, but my question is this: what are you going to do about it?

Where have you seen Jesus show up recently?

11

OBEDIENCE

Then Moses rose early in the morning and went up Mount Sinai, as the LORD had commanded him.

—EXODUS 34:4 (NKJV)

If you remember, I have been reading through the Old Testament. No disrespect to God's Word, but that can get boring fast—all those laws, regulations, genealogies. As I was closing Exodus and heading into Leviticus, this one phrase kept coming up: "just as the Lord commanded."

That sounds simple. Like, duh, we're Christians, therefore we do what God says. Hmmm, but do we really? Think about it. I cannot count how many times God nudged me to move, but I rebelled and stood still. Am I ashamed of that? Yes. Does God forgive me for that? Also, yes. We often think about God like one of our parents, the one who gets angry and blows up the minute we even begin to disobey. I truly believe that God is not like that at all. He knows we're not perfect, yet He loves us anyway. He just wants us to try. He wants us to trust Him, to take His hand and say yes. Are we going to mess up? Absolutely. One of my favorite authors, Bob Goff, wrote in his book *Everybody Always*, "God doesn't grimace at our failures, He delights in our attempts."[1]

What do you need to do to obey God today?

---

[1] Goff, B., 2018. *Everybody, Always.* [Place of publication not identified]: Thomas Nelson, p.66.

12

FOLLOW GOD

*A man's heart plans his way, but
the LORD directs his steps.*

—PROVERBS 16:9 (NKJV)

First, I *love* Proverbs, so I highly suggest you read it. All of it. Every word.

Anyway, that is not my point for today.

I made the tough decision to leave my church this week. I grew up in that church, just like my mom did, and her dad before her. My grandfather literally gave his life in service of that church. To say leaving was a difficult decision is an understatement. I had been praying about this situation for months. Last Sunday night, I realized enough was enough. I cried *a lot*. God met me there and reminded me that I shouldn't have to sacrifice my relationship with Him to please a few people. I met with my pastor and left.

This Sunday, I decided to attend the Church of the Highlands campus in Tuscaloosa. I had been to the one in Birmingham many times before and loved it, so why not, right? I've prayed this whole week about a new church home. I knew I was obedient in leaving so I knew God was going to provide. Honestly, I did not expect to be smacked in the face with a sign as soon as I sat down.

My mom and I were sitting there, three rows back, first two seats. A young woman, who is a greeter at the church, came up, shook our hands, and said, "Good morning. I'm Laney. Where are y'all from?" Mom answered Fayette and so Laney told us that she is from Cullman. Wait. What? You mean, where I am about to live for college Cullman? Hang on, the story isn't over.

My mom proceeded to point to me and told Laney that I would be living up there and going to Wallace State. Laney said, "Oh I love Wallace. What are you going to study?"

I told her I would be in the occupational therapy assistant program. She replied, "No way! My dad is an OT, and he works at" so and so company. "So, let me know if you need a connection." I am not kidding at all. When she walked away, I was thinking, *Okay, wow. If that's not a sign, I don't know what is.*

God works in mysterious ways. Sometimes we can't even see where we're going when He tells us to move. Trust me, He knows best, even when it seems too wild to be real. That's just how God works. Do yourself a favor and say yes to anything He tells you.

Reflect on a time when God revealed Himself to you in a supernatural way.

13

REDEMPTION

⌄⌄

*"The LORD repay your work, and a full reward
be given you by the LORD God of Israel, under
whose wings you have come for refuge."*

—RUTH 2:12 (NKJV)

⌃⌃

To be honest, I put off writing for longer than I should have. I haven't felt close to God or even sure I've heard Him clearly in a few weeks. I did my devotions, read my Bible, read my Christian books, prayed; I did all the things a "good Christian girl" is supposed to do. Still, I felt lonely, confused, far away.

Out of nowhere one night, a friend of mine texted me a paragraph about how he had been feeling the exact same way I had. We exchanged the typical church lingo like "Oh, be intentional. Pray more. Read more. It'll all be fine." Well, if that was true, then why didn't I feel fine? After all, I'd been doing all the same things I just told him to do. What was going on with me?

Finally, after a couple days, I'd had enough. I said, "God, I've been putting my flesh above You. I want to focus on You and only You. I miss you. You've been quiet for too long. Help me hear You." There was no mysterious booming voice, no blinding light, no clap of thunder like I expected. It was simply quiet. A passage from a book I had just finished crossed my mind. It was something about how it's not about our works, but His grace. I picked up my Bible and started reading where I left off: the book of Ruth. Ironically, that happens to be a book about how redemption has nothing to do with the redeemed; the redeemer himself does all the work. It was like the floodgates had opened. Tears began streaming down my face and I realized that my hardest, most pure efforts would fail every time. It's about embracing the incredible gift of the Redeemer who did all the work to bring me out of the darkness and into joyous light.

Don't cheapen grace by making it about what you're doing. It is only through the sacrifice of the Redeemer that we may have life. Thank God for His grace!

Have you been going through the motions or truly embracing God's grace this week?

14

JESUS TOOK OUR PLACE

⩔

And when Jesus came to the place, He looked up and saw him, and said to him, "Zacchaeus, make haste and come down, for today I must stay at your house."

—LUKE 19:5 (NKJV)

⩓

If you grew up in church, then you know the story of Zacchaeus, the wee little man in a tree. He worked as a tax collector. This meant that he was a rich, lying, cheater who everyone despised. Zacchaeus wanted to figure out who this Jesus man was, but because he was hated so much, he was pushed to the back of the crowd. Since he was short, he couldn't see, so he climbed a tree.

Fortunately, Jesus sees hated sinners like Zacchaeus. They often look like you and me. He loves them and wants to make them whole, make them righteous. In order to do that though, Jesus had to take the cruel punishment that should have been ours to bear: the crucifixion. He loves us so much that He took our ugly, sinful identities and gave us new, spotless ones. To God, we are now blameless because Jesus took our place.

Why was Zacchaeus in the tree? Because he was despised. Jesus would end His earthly ministry hung on a tree in ridicule. Jesus called Zacchaeus down from a place of shame and into the place of honor, and took Zacchaeus's place on the tree.

Think of a time when you were pushed to the back of the crowd like Zacchaeus. Do you have enough faith to climb the tree if you're ever in that situation again?

15

HEART POSTURE

*Then the people rejoiced, for they had offered willingly,
because with a loyal heart they had offered willingly
to the LORD; and King David also rejoiced greatly.*

—1 CHRONICLES 29:9 (NKJV)

The summer of 2020 was supposed to be the sixth in a row that I had gone to a church camp called Super Summer. I remember that very first year so vividly. My eyes were wide with wonder and excitement, and my mind was ready to soak up all the new information I would hear that week. That awe remained every single summer. I can recall multiple tear-filled worship services where the presence of God felt so near, I could touch it. There were also times when I didn't feel anything. I wanted to so badly—or at least I thought I did.

I'd force myself to raise my hands in hope of coercing a closeness with God, but there was nothing. In those moments, I felt so defeated, like something was wrong with me. Over the years though, I've learned that you can't force God to do anything. God is holy. Of course He isn't going to blow me away with His Spirit if my heart is saying, "Look at that guy over there. He is so cute *and* he's worshipping Jesus. Wow!" God won't fight for your attention.

A youth pastor once reminded me that our worship experience reflects our posture. This is not just the state our bodies are in, hands stretched to heaven, but also the state our hearts are in, open and willing to hear the whispers of our God. Listen, it's okay to not be moved to tears every time you hear a Christian song. But when you're intentionally seeking the presence of the Lord, be willing to hear whatever He has to say, whether you like it or not. Ultimately, you will rejoice because God will allow you to realize that He is your true source of joy and He knows best.

When was the last time you entered God's presence with an open and willing heart?

16

ANSWERED PRAYERS

"The hand of our God is upon all those for good who seek Him, but His wrath and power are against all those who forsake Him." So we fasted and entreated our God for this, and He answered our prayer.

—EZRA 8:22-23 (NKJV)

I don't believe in unanswered prayers. I think God *always* answers. Sometimes, it's just not the answer we want. There are times when God says yes, and there are times when God says no. Trust me, looking back, there are so many things I prayed for that I'm beyond thankful that God said no to. If God had given me everything I thought I wanted, I would be stuck in a cycle of hurtful, abusive, and manipulative relationships.

Now you may be wondering about another verse that says ask, seek, knock, and all will be given to you (Matthew 7:7–8 NKJV). Well, here's the thing: God wants what is best for you. When your heart and mind are aligned with His, you will naturally ask for God's best, also known as His will. On the other hand, God may decide to give you what you thought you wanted to show you that it is not at all what you needed.

Just be honest with God. Don't get mad at Him when He tells you no or not yet. Trust that He sees the bigger picture and you shall never be in lack when you are seeking Him above all else. Talk to God. He wants to hear from you.

If you are brave enough, pray for God's will instead of your own this week and see what happens.

17

ATTRIBUTES OF GOD

"They refused to obey, and they were not mindful of Your wonders that You did among them. But they hardened their necks, and in their rebellion, they appointed a leader to return to their bondage. But You are God, ready to pardon, gracious and merciful, slow to anger, abundant in kindness, and did not forsake them."

—NEHEMIAH 9:17 (NKJV)

God has innumerable characteristics, but I can think of no better one to focus on than His mercy. According to the Oxford Learner's dictionary, *mercy* is defined as compassion or forgiveness shown toward someone who is within one's power to punish or harm. I want you to take a moment and really acknowledge what mercy means.

We serve a God who is so holy, so righteous, so all-powerful that He could (and probably should) wipe every aspect of life off the face of the planet in a snap. That should scare you. It terrifies me (a healthy fear, mind you). While God is fearfully all-powerful, He is also all loving and all merciful. I encourage you to read all of Nehemiah chapter 9. You will see that the Israelites are just like us. They turned away from God and broke every commandment more times than I can count. God had every right to strike them, to punish them. He is God and they disobeyed. Yet, every single time they showed a hint of remorse, and even when they didn't, God rushed in and overwhelmed them with His abundant mercy.

They doubted Him, but He showed up anyway. They disobeyed Him, but He guided them anyway. They turned away from Him, but He delivered them anyway. They worshipped everything but Him, but He loved them anyway. They committed every sin and they all deserved death, but He poured out His mercy anyway.

I don't know about you, but that gets me emotional. Nothing you can ever do will separate you from God because the ultimate mercy happened on the cross. Jesus, the perfect Son of God, took our shame, our sin, and our punishment upon Himself and paid our ransom. He defeated sin. He defeated death. He is standing up there at the right hand of God, holding the keys to Hell and He is saying, "You don't have to suffer anymore, because I've already done it for you."

After knowing all that, how can we not give Him everything we have and devote our hearts and lives to Him? Thank God for His mercy!

How does knowing this change the way you view God?

18
WAIT FOR IT

Wait on the LORD; be of good courage, and He shall strengthen your heart; wait, I say, on the LORD.

—PSALM 27:14 (NKJV)

I made myself memorize this verse in 2017. I would repeat it over and over again whenever I started to worry or be anxious. It calmed me down. However, it wasn't until recently that the truth of this verse really penetrated my heart.

I am not a patient person. I hate waiting. I told myself that I would never pray for patience because I knew God would give me circumstances to be patient, and I didn't want to do that. As I've grown, I started praying that God would search me and mold me, whatever the cost. It is a dangerous prayer I know, but I desperately wanted to connect to God on a deeper level.

Then the coronavirus pandemic happened in 2020. Guess what? I had to wait on seeing my friends. I had to wait on my senior year activities. I had to wait to see my brother and sister. I had to wait for graduation. As all these overwhelming thoughts and feelings came upon me, I prayed harder than I ever have before. God reminded me to stay positive because something good was just around the corner. I don't know what all this promised good is going to include, but I can already see deeper friendships, stronger faith, more complete trust in God, and growing passion to do God's will.

Even after all of that, I'm still waiting. Waiting on a boyfriend. Waiting on college. Waiting to move out. Waiting on trips. That's okay, because I know God is giving me the strength and virtue to be patient. Do I always have a good attitude about it? Absolutely not. But that's okay too, because God is right there beside me saying, "You are going to be blown away at what's coming. You'll be so glad I made you wait."

Think of something that you really wanted but had to wait for. How much more did you appreciate it once you got it?

19

YOUR STORY ISN'T OVER

So it was, as the multitude pressed about Him [Jesus] to hear the word of God, that He stood by the Lake of Gennesaret, and saw two boats standing by the lake; but the fishermen had gone from them and were washing their nets. Then He got into one of the boats, which was Simon's, and asked him to put out a little from the land. And He sat down and taught the multitudes from the boat. When He had stopped speaking, He said to Simon, "Launch out into the deep and let down your nets for a catch." But Simon answered and said to Him, "Master, we have toiled all night and caught nothing; nevertheless, at Your word I will let down the net." And when they had done this, they caught a great number of fish, and their net was breaking. So they signaled to their partners in the other boat to come and help them. And they came and filled both boats, so that they began to sink. When Simon Peter saw it, he fell down at Jesus' knees saying, "Depart from me for I am a sinful man, O Lord!" For he and all who were with him were astonished at the catch of fish which they had taken; and so also were James and John, the sons of Zebedee, who were partners with Simon. And Jesus said to Simon, "Do not be afraid. From now of you will catch men." So when they had brought their boats to land, they forsook all and followed Him

—LUKE 5:1–11 (NKJV)

I know what you're thinking: "Oh great, another fisher of men story that I've heard a thousand times. I'm supposed to follow Jesus and tell others about Him. Yeah I know." While this is the fisher of men passage of scripture, I want to call your attention to the punctuation. Any English teacher will stress the importance of punctuation when writing. Punctuation in the Bible is no different. Every comma, colon, and semicolon serves a purpose. Specifically, let's focus on verse 5 and its semicolon: "But Simon answered and said to Him, 'Master, we have toiled all night and caught nothing; nevertheless at Your word I will let down the net'" (Luke 5:5 NKJV).

A semicolon is defined as a punctuation mark indicating a pause, typically between two main clauses, that is more pronounced than that indicated by a comma. You see, Simon could have ended his story saying, "Look dude, we've been fishing all night and there's nothing to catch. Give it up and go home." But thankfully for him, he felt something was different about this man they called Jesus. Simon took a moment to pause and reflect and decided to obey the word of Jesus. As you read above, his life was forever changed because of this encounter.

Everyone has a semicolon moment in his or her life—that pause, that moment when the knocking on our heart's door is louder than ever before and we walk toward it, turn the knob, and let Jesus in. Once you encounter Jesus, everything changes.

There are plenty more examples of this throughout Scripture. In Genesis 17, Abram and Sarai encountered God and He changed their names to Abraham and Sarah. In Genesis 32, Jacob physically wrestled with God and walked with a limp for the rest of his life. In Acts 9, Saul encountered Jesus, was blinded, and had his name changed to Paul. Understand that when we truly encounter our Holy and Awesome God, our lives will never look the same, but the change is always for the better. One of my favorite authors, Lysa TerKeurst, says this in her book *It's Not Supposed to Be This Way*: "We trust a God who allows hurt. But we also trust a God who uses hurt for good."[2]

How amazing is that? Just because your past is riddled with sin, mistakes, failures, shame, and running full force away from God does not disqualify you from His Grace or Salvation. God wants to take the sentence of your life and add a semicolon to it. Your story does not end with all your bad but starts there to show the rest of the world the redemptive power of the God we serve. Make the decision to follow Jesus. Your life will never be the same. If you're still questioning, always

---

[2] TerKeurst, L., 2018. *It's not supposed to be this way.* Thomas Nelson, p.227.

remember this: don't put a period where God wants to put a semicolon.

―――――――――

How can you share the story of your semicolon
moment with someone this week?

20

WALK WITH HIM

Now by this we know that we know Him, if we keep His commandments. He who says, "I know Him," and does not keep His commandments, is a liar, and the truth is not in him. But whoever keeps His word, truly the love of God is perfected in him. By this we know that we are in Him. He who says he abides in Him ought himself also to walk just as He walked.

—1 JOHN 2:3-6 (NKJV)

After reading these verses, you may be wondering how in the world it is possible to always obey Jesus. With humans and their sinful nature, asking for 100 percent obedience 100 percent of the time is a tall order. Doesn't the Bible say that God is forgiving? If that's true, then why is John so bold in calling us liars if we happen to mess up?

Here's the thing: Jesus knows that we're not perfect. We will never be able to imitate Him completely this side of eternity. Jesus also knows that we cannot encounter Him without being changed. When we accept Christ as our salvation, we undergo a complete heart renovation. Our motives are no longer success-seeking and self-serving. Our actions will reflect, though often imperfectly, the actions of our Lord because we are now motivated by His love, His grace, and His calling on our lives.

As for the liar part, John is not saying that if you mess up then you don't really know the saving power of Jesus. He is saying that the liars are the ones who think good works and church attendance is what saves them. They can claim to know Jesus all they want, but it's only a head knowledge. They haven't experienced heart and life transformation, and therefore, their motives are not rooted in the Word of God.

Don't stress over trying to be the perfect Christ follower. It simply isn't possible. Just be obedient to

Jesus in the very next step. Then the next. And the next. Following Jesus is a walk, not a sprint. Don't make yourself winded with trying in your own strength. Follow His lead and watch how far you can go.

How can you say yes to God today?

21

LET ME DOWN

*It is better to trust in the LORD than to put
confidence in men. It is better to trust in the
LORD than to put confidence in princes.*

—PSALM 118:8–9 (NKJV)

If you are like me, you like to be the one in control. It can be difficult to trust others to give you a hand. While there's nothing wrong with working hard and doing things yourself, it becomes a problem when we work ourselves so hard that we're left exhausted and stressed to the max. Even then, it may be hard to trust and let others in. Why? Because people will let you down. None of us is perfect or capable of doing it all. God, on the other hand, is amazingly perfect. He always fulfills His promises, and the strength He gives surpasses all understanding.

Again, if you're like me, you're probably thinking, "Well, if I put my trust in God, what if He asks me to do something and I let Him down?" Trust me, I get it. No one wants to let others down or feel like a failure. Here is the incredible, freeing truth: it is impossible for you to let God down because you were never the one holding Him up in the first place. God is the one holding you when you trust in Him, and the Bible gives us countless stories as evidence that God will never let us down. Rest in that truth today.

Reflect on a time when you reluctantly trusted God with something, and He ended up exceeding your expectations.

22

OVERWHELMED

When my spirit was overwhelmed within me, then You knew my path. In the way in which I walk...

—PSALM 142:3 (NKJV)

God spoke to me with this verse when I needed it most. The previous week had been wild, but in a good way. I graduated, I turned 18, I spent time laughing with my dearest friends. However, as I'm writing this, I just feel stuck and tired. Physically tired, yes, but also mentally and emotionally tired. Tired of not having answers. Tired of no organization. Tired of waiting. I am just drained and distraught. Honestly, I have no idea what my future will look like with the world in the state that it's in. There are so many things I want that I can't have yet.

Thankfully, we serve a God who draws near in times of need, especially our greatest ones. He reminded me that even though I feel done and tired, He knows where my journey leads. He knows what amazing things He has in store. This is so encouraging! When I want to quit, God reminds me to rely on His strength and omniscience. It's okay to feel down. Just don't stay there.

Following God is not always easy. In fact, it is often difficult. That's why we must keep our eyes fixed on Him. When we do that, all the hard times and pain pale in comparison to the reward that is to come.

Are you willing to ask God for help?

23

JUST LIKE JESUS

He has shown you, O man, what is good; and what does the LORD require of you but to do justly, to love mercy, and to walk humbly with your God?

—MICAH 6:8 (NKJV)

One of the things that has hit me hardest this season is a simple phrase from one of my favorite Elevation Worship songs, "Here Again," which is "not for a minute was I forsaken." I think we get so caught up in trying to live the "perfect" Christian life. We are rushing around and being so hard on ourselves trying to please God, not sin, and act in ways that are holy and righteous. In reality, Jesus just asked us to follow Him. There is no overnight transformation miracle from cussing sailor to proper English professor. It requires some sacrifice. It is a process. It is a journey. There are going to be tough times that wear us thin. All God really wants from us is our hearts. He wants us to obey, to try, to love. It is not as difficult as we make it out to be.

The difficult part is embracing the gospel. Believe that there is a God whose love is so miraculous that He knew every wretched thing we would ever do and still chose to die for us. Believe that there is a God who willingly swaps places with us so we may be seen as pure and whole instead of dirty and broken. Believe that there is a God who, when we say, "No, I deserve this," looks at us with tears in His eyes and says, "Give me your sins, my child." Accept that there is nothing we can do to earn anything; it is all God.

TRANSPARENCY

Could it be true? All He asks for in return is for us to love Him. Sounds like an amazing deal to me.

---

*Pray for God to expand your capacity to
love and understanding of His truth.*

24

THE FORGIVENESS PROCESS

Let all bitterness, wrath, anger, clamor, and evil speaking be put away from you, with all malice. And be kind to one another, tenderhearted, forgiving one another, even as God in Christ forgave you.

—EPHESIANS 4:31–32 (NKJV)

I'm writing this at 8:30 at night on December 28 of 2020. To say this year has been unprecedented would be an understatement. I can't even begin to unpack everything that I've experienced and learned this year, but God has laid a word so heavily on my heart tonight—a word that He wants me to share with you. I started my first semester of OTA (occupational therapy assistant) school in August. It's been amazing and I've loved every minute, even the tear-filled study sessions. This semester has also been the lowest season of my life. I moved out of my parents' home and lived in a one-bedroom apartment by myself. Sure, I spoke to my friends and family daily, but the feelings of loneliness became overwhelming. I tried to stay on top of my Bible reading, tried to keep up the appearances of being a good Christian. God felt so distant, and I felt so alone. Eventually, depression became my roommate. Not many people knew. It took a while for me to even admit it to my two best friends, to whom I tell everything. I went through the motions and wore two masks every day: one to comply with COVID regulations, and the other depicting a fake smile. I was pretending that everything was okay. Being one who enjoys having control, I have no other explanation but the prompting of the Holy Spirit for me winding up in the campus counselor's office. I didn't know where to begin. I didn't even know what to say.

I'll admit, I was highly skeptical. Guess what? I was in counseling for six weeks. There was so much unresolved hurt and offense that I had pushed down so far, I wasn't even aware it was still burdening me. My counselor, a Christian man himself, guided me in processing my pain and eventually reaching a point where I was ready to forgive my offenders—really forgive them. I had claimed I had done that already, but it was just another mask I had put on to seem like a good Christian. Walking out of his office that sixth week felt weird. I felt oddly free, light, and full of expectation. I was ready to move forward and build healthy, lasting relationships. I was ready to no longer allow the enemy to keep me down by bringing up my past. The only past that I wanted to dwell on was the work Jesus did on the cross to forgive everything I've ever done and will do, and to forgive all the things my offenders have done too. I'll explain more about my experience in counseling later in this book. Experiencing the freedom of forgiveness is no easy feat. It's not something that happens at the altar one time and you're good. It's a process. It's a lesson you learn and practice over and over and over again. Now, for the first time in a long time, I can actually say I'm happy. I'm still actively seeking God and strengthening that relationship. I'm still actively changing my mindset to forgive and to practice healthy coping mechanisms, and that's okay. Life's a journey, so lean in and let God take your hand.

Who do you need to start the process of forgiveness with this week?

25

GROPING AFTER GOD

"His purpose was for the nations to seek after God and perhaps feel their way toward him and find him—though he is not far from any one of us."

—ACTS 17:27 (NLT)

Some translations of this verse use the phrase "that they might grope for Him and find Him." *Grope* is defined as the action of feeling about or searching blindly or uncertainly with your hands. It's like when your alarm goes off in the morning and you're hitting everything on your nightstand hoping to eventually hit that snooze button. Another example that's more personal for me is when I'm hit with a sudden migraine and I'm feeling my way through the medicine cabinet in hopes of coming across some Excedrin to lessen my pain. Whether we realize it or not, we are all constantly searching for something: something to make us happy, something to fill the void, something to numb the pain, something to make us feel important or included. We grope after all these material things in our vain efforts to fill a hole in our hearts that we just can't seem to understand.

Some of us may have a story where we searched for all the wrong things and finally stumbled upon Jesus. That is incredible and your story is just as important as anyone else's. On the other hand, some of us may have had an idea of Jesus and intentionally searched for Him. Please don't misunderstand me or the verse above. We should be mindful and intentional about seeking after God. Luke, the author of the book of Acts, is not instructing us to be blind and uncertain in our pursuits for Jesus. What I believe he is hinting at is that we should be constantly feeling our way toward Jesus subconsciously. We should be seeking after God and being obedient to His will so faithfully and fervently that we don't really have to dwell on thinking about it. It's no longer something we have to mull over; the action of following God should become second nature.

Here's another way of looking at it. When you are following the plan God has for your life, it is not always going to be easy, simple, or even bright. Sometimes we have to walk through rocky valleys and darkness. What do we do when we are walking in a dark place? We use our hands to feel our way through. When we are confident that God is good and we are chasing after His good plan, we can also be confident when we are groping around in the tough times. He is going to give us what we need to get through. Sometimes provision is not immediate. Sometimes we wait so long that we are almost certain that this dark place will be our new home. That is when we must be diligent in searching for God. God is not far from us. In fact, He's right next to us all the time. If we can just have enough faith to reach out our hands, God will show us the way through.

What is it that you've been searching for?

26

MENTAL HEALTH
AND THE CHURCH

Be anxious for nothing, but in everything by prayer and supplication, with thanksgiving, let your requests be made known to God; and the peace of God, which surpasses all understanding, will guard your hearts and minds through Christ Jesus.

—PHILIPPIANS 4:6–7 (NKJV)

Philippians is one of the most quoted books of the New Testament. I would dare bet that even if you didn't grow up in a Christian home, you probably heard verses like Philippians 4:13 quoted before some sporting event or competition. While this isn't wrong or a bad thing, I think it's important to understand the context behind the verses we tend to throw around. Philippians is considered the book of joy. In fact, the word "joy" or "rejoice" is repeated over a dozen times throughout the short four-chapter book. What is most fascinating to me about this is that Paul wrote this letter to the Church at Philippi from a jail cell. Paul was in the middle of his first Roman imprisonment and authored arguably the happiest and most encouraging book in the Bible.

I don't know about you, but if I was behind bars, I think I would be everything but happy and joyful. How can this be? My answer is that he was focused more on God than his circumstances. However, that's the problem, isn't it? Our circumstances can look scary and so overwhelming that we feel as if we're in a prison of our own. Often we feel that God is so silent, or we've been running for so long, that our problems look a lot bigger than God. Let me take a minute here to say that feelings are not facts and faith is not a feeling; faith is a decision.

To be quite honest, I think that the modern-day church has done a poor job of talking about mental health. As much as I am ashamed to admit, I used to share in the belief that if people would just pray more or go to church more then they wouldn't be so anxious or depressed. God never said that we wouldn't face storms, but He did promise to be right there with us when we did. Accepting Christ doesn't automatically make your life perfect and more joyful—quite the opposite actually. Yes, accepting Christ does give you peace and a joy that is not of this earth, but it also makes life vastly more complicated. Jesus promised us in the book of John that since He was persecuted, we would be too. In the fall of 2020, I was entering my first semester of OTA school. I was living on my own, almost two hours away from my family, and it was great for a while, as I've mentioned before. Then I started to spiral. I was lonely, isolated, and downright sad. I never believed that me, a girl who was baptized at seven years old, would be struggling with depression. I sat in my apartment alone and cried for more nights than I care to admit. I struggled with thoughts of insecurities, doubts, fears, anger, and cried out a particular set of questions quite often: "God, why am I feeling this way? What is wrong with me?" I believe that God will always meet you where you are if you invite Him. The problem that fueled the flames of my depression was that God seemed so silent. I cried out over and over again with seemingly no answer. I was frustrated and confused and doubted my salvation. Then I found a paper in my student handbook about an assignment that would be due in the spring. We had to visit a counselor and have him sign something for our mental health class. Being the overachiever that I am, I went ahead and booked an appointment with the campus counselor so I could check off this assignment months before it was due. I had every intention of just going the one time I had to. I walked into the counselor's office with the belief that shrinks were just there to feed you shallow answers to your questions and get a paycheck. They were people who had a job because society didn't pray enough to resolve their issues. Boy was I wrong. I left that appointment an hour later with tears streaming down my face and a standing weekly appointment for as long as I needed. God finally opened my eyes to the fact that I had not dealt with hurts from past relationships with guys in high school and my relationship with my own father. I was still white knuckling these deep-rooted pains that I hadn't released at the feet of Jesus. I met with the counselor for six weeks. Finally, I was starting to feel peace and freedom. This counselor challenged me to write what is called a "love letter," which ultimately allowed me to confront the hurts that had held me down for so long and forgive those men, sincerely. (I have attached an outline of the "love letter" in the back of this book in hopes that you too can find freedom.) God used this precious counselor to be His mouthpiece and speak life, love, peace, forgiveness, and joy into my soul in one of the darkest moments in my life. Experiencing depression or anxiety doesn't mean you're not a "good Christian." It's okay to ask for help. Yes, pray to God and seek Him with all your heart, but God also put counselors and therapists here for a reason. He can use these professionals to speak to your heart just like He did mine. There is no shame in admitting you struggle with mental health. Seek God, the ultimate Healer and Provider, but don't let others convince you that seeking professional help makes you less than. In my opinion, it makes you stronger.

Ironically, the counselor accepted a job in a different state and his last day was two days after my last appointment. Because of this and the fact that the college hadn't yet found a replacement when spring rolled around, that assignment was discarded. Some might say that I went for nothing, but to me it was nothing short of divine intervention.

What steps do I need to take this week to get healthy mentally?

27

UNCERTAIN TIMES

"Don't be afraid of them, for the LORD your God fights for you."

—DEUTERONOMY 3:22 (HCSB)

I am writing this in late August of 2021. A new variant of the COVID-19 virus has surfaced, vaccines are being mandated in some places, and one was just FDA approved. In other words, my future is uncertain. I have graduated college with my OTA degree and am still waiting to receive my score from the board exam. In the waiting, the doubts start to creep in. Will I still have a job if I decide to remain unvaccinated? What if I didn't pass? Will I have to quit my job? What will I choose if I have to make that hard decision? Will I be able to provide for myself?

My best friend texted me earlier today and told me she decided to drop nursing school, even though she is halfway through, and this has been her dream for as long as she can remember. Vaccines are being mandated to finish certain clinical hours, and she doesn't feel peace about getting the vaccine and shouldn't be forced to get it. Wow. I have so much respect for this girl. I cannot imagine how tough this decision was, but knowing her for as long as I have, I know this decision was covered in prayer before it was set in stone. She's uncertain of her future, but she knows that God is calling her to bigger things, scary things—things that required her to set aside the dream she's had since she was a little girl. I don't know if I'll be the next one faced with this decision, and to be honest I am still unsure of what I would choose. Worry and doubt has flooded my mind today. I know with every fiber of my being that God is in control, and He will provide. However, it's still so hard when the world is as broken as it is today and there are so many opinions being thrown at you. I went to the bathroom to get some tissues to wipe the tears streaming down my face. I stopped and looked in the mirror and I said, "God I trust your plan, help me with my unbelief. Use me however you see fit." Now I know this is a risky prayer because there is potential for God to ask me to give up all I've worked for thus far. Not ten minutes after this, I started scrolling through Facebook and I saw a post that pierced my heart. I knew without a doubt it was God speaking to me. It read, "The devil wants you to worry about what's next so you can't enjoy what's now. The devil is a liar. Stop worrying. Always focus on God and enjoy every single day He has given."

I don't have a neat and tidy ending to this devotion. I don't have answers about my future, and I probably won't get them until right before I need them. I do know that God hears me, He loves me, and He has something so much better in store for all those who love Him. Sure, it's scary and my controlling tendencies call me to worry. But God calls me to trust and have peace because He is fighting for me.

What is your attitude toward God during uncertain times?

28

THE COMPASSION
OF JESUS

⌄

When they had eaten breakfast, Jesus asked Simon Peter, "Simon, son of John, do you love me more than these?" "Yes, Lord," he said to him, "you know that I love you." "Feed my lambs," he told him. A second time he asked him, "Simon, son of John, do you love me?" "Yes, Lord," he said to him, "you know that I love you." "Shepherd my sheep," he told him. He asked him the third time, "Simon, son of John, do you love me?" Peter was grieved that he asked him the third time, "Do you love me?" He said, "Lord, you know everything; you know that I love you." "Feed my sheep," Jesus said.

—JOHN 21:15–17 (HCSB)

⌃

If you grew up in church like me, then you probably heard that Jesus asked Peter three times because Peter had denied Jesus three times. I'm not saying that this statement is wrong. These verses do, in fact, show Jesus' beautiful threefold restoration of Peter. There is also more evidence here of the compassion of Jesus that we can't get from the English translations; we must go to the original Greek. In English, we only have one word for love, but the Greeks, being so much more articulate and passionate than we, have four. There is *storge*, meaning an empathy bond, *philia* or *phileo*, meaning a friendly or brotherly love (this is why Philadelphia is called the city of brotherly love), *eros*, meaning a romantic love, and *agape*, which is an unconditional God love.

The first two times Jesus asked, he used the word *agape* which, as we just learned, is the sacrificial, unconditional love of God. Peter only ever used the word *phileo*, the friendly, brotherly love. The last time Jesus asked, He used *phileo* instead of *agape*. Now you're probably wondering why this even matters or how this is significant. This shows that Jesus, instead of asking for something that we, as finite, fallible human beings could never accomplish on this side of eternity, lowered the expectation to meet us where we are. How beautiful is that. Jesus knew that Peter only understood brotherly love at this point in his life.

He knew that this conversation was giving Peter just another glimpse at the *agape* love of God. God, once again, lowered Himself to bring us up into true, right relationship with Him.

***

How does this shift your perspective of the personality of Jesus?

29

SYMBOLISM OF THE SEASON

⋙

Then she gave birth to her first-born son, and she wrapped him tightly in cloth and laid him in a manger, because there was no guest room available for them.

—LUKE 2:7 (CSB)

Then they opened their treasures and presented him with gifts: gold, frankincense, and myrrh.

—MATTHEW 2:11 (CSB)

As I write this, I'm sipping coffee surrounded by the soft glow of Christmas tree lights. Christmas is always a special time filled with Santa and gifts and over-the-top light displays. But I often feel as if the point of Christmas, Jesus, gets suppressed more and more each year as we fall into the trap of consumerism. I'm sure you've heard, or more likely have seen plastered on Hobby Lobby décor, the saying, "Jesus is the reason for the season." While this saying is one hundred percent true, I don't think we fully understand the true weight of the statement.

Some of us may have the tradition of gathering around to read the Christmas story with our families or attend live nativities with our church. These activities are incredible ways to keep Jesus at the forefront of our minds during the holidays, so I'm not discrediting their importance. What I do believe, though, is that we gloss over the details. These details are what speak to the majesty and wonder of Christ's birth. Let me show you what I mean. Above, I gave you two verses from two accounts of the Savior's birth recorded in the gospels of Matthew and Luke. I highly encourage you to read through the whole story to get the full picture, but these verses have some incredible details that we so often overlook.

To understand these details, we must study the Jewish customs of the time, especially those surrounding the death and burial of loved ones. When a Jewish person died, the first step the family took was preparing the body. This included washing the body, anointing the body with perfumes and spices, and wrapping the body with strips of cloth. Look again at the verses we read above. Baby Jesus was wrapped in cloth and one of the three gifts He was given was myrrh, an ingredient commonly used as embalming oil to anoint the body of the deceased. Within moments of Jesus's birth, His purpose is being proclaimed. The minute He entered this world, He was already being prepared for His death. The other two gifts are equally as profound. Gold represented his royalty—a gift symbolizing His kingship here on earth. Finally, there is frankincense, an incense that symbolized His deity. A passage from *Contra Celsum,* a major apologetics work written by the Church Father Origen of Alexandria around AD 248, reads, "gold, as to a king; myrrh, as to one who was mortal; and incense, as to a God."[3] I hope that your perspective of the Christmas story is starting to shift.

Now, there is the fact that Jesus was laid in a manger. By definition, a manger is a trough for horses or cattle to eat from. You may be thinking, "Well Kylie,

---

[3] En.wikipedia.org. 2022. *Biblical Magi - Wikipedia.* [online] Available at: <https://en.wikipedia.org/wiki/Biblical_Magi#:~:text=The%20three%20gifts%20had%20a,%2C%20as%20to%20a%20God.%22> [Accessed 16 July 2022].

Jesus was born in a stable with animals, so the options were slim." While this observation is correct, God does everything on purpose. I am reminded of one of Jesus's seven "I am" statements from the book of John. John 6:35 (NKJV) records Jesus saying, "I am the bread of life." In other words, the bread of life was born in a food trough. Let that sink in.

There are so many details throughout that Bible that point us to who Jesus is and how incredible His wonders are. It would take years for us to unpack them all, and quite honestly there are many that I'm still discovering. Let's read these familiar stories again with a fresh understanding.

How has Jesus impacted the details of your life?

30

WHAT GOD WANTS

"She has done what she could; she has anointed my body in advance for burial."

—MARK 14:8 (HCSB)

This verse is from the famous story of Jesus's anointing at Bethany. A sinful woman crashes the party to cover the Savior with expensive perfume and her own tears. Jesus Himself promised the story would be told until the end of time. If you're unfamiliar with the story, I encourage you to read it for yourself, but today I'll give you the highlights. Jesus was at a dinner party when this woman showed up uninvited. She broke this alabaster jar of perfume and drenched Jesus over the head. This was no ordinary perfume; this perfume was worth more than 300 denarii, which was the equivalent of over a year's wages. Some scholars believe that this pricey fragrance could have very well been her dowry, so it was a great sacrifice to give it up. Other guests at this party began to criticize her act of obedience to God, claiming this perfume could be sold and the money given to the poor. Then Jesus piped up. Jesus defended this woman's actions because Jesus knew her heart. The story ends by saying that this encounter prompted Judas to begin the process of betraying Jesus.

Now that we're on the same page, I want to clarify something. Jesus was not implying that he did not care about the poor. Because of the depravity of sin and human nature, poverty will always be an issue; it is something that cannot be eradicated. Jesus saw the hearts of these critics. They didn't care about the poor, and their greed spoke volumes about the condition of their spiritual lives. We will always criticize that which we don't understand. These men didn't understand this woman's act of worship. They didn't understand loving Jesus so much that giving Him all that you had still didn't seem like enough. I also want to bring attention to the fact that the woman broke the jar. After all, it is a jar and jars are made to pour without being broken. However, don't our greatest moments of worship and surrender to God happen when we feel most broken? Pastor Rich Wilkerson Jr. from VOUS Church out of Miami, Florida says that "worshipping God is never wasteful. In fact, anything not offered to God in worship is a waste. Like the broken alabaster jar, you've been broken greatly so God can use you powerfully." We must remember that broken jars still pour.

In John's account of this encounter, we learn who this woman is (John 12:1–8 HCSB). This woman is Mary, the sister of Martha and Lazarus—yes, the same Lazarus Jesus resurrected after four days. This is significant because the Jews believed that after three days of being dead, your soul leaves your body. In other words, Lazarus was *dead* dead. Mary had a story. Mary had seen firsthand the mighty works of God in her own life. Mary was the one who wrote to Jesus when Lazarus was sick, saying, "the one you love is sick" (John 11:3 HCSB). Mary was the one who wept with the Savior. Mary didn't plead with Jesus or beg him to come; she appealed to His compassion, His heart. With her alabaster jar of perfume, Mary demonstrated an unconventional, unashamed expression of love for Jesus. She gave Him her heart, which is all He's ever wanted from each of us.

I'll leave you with one last thought. This anointing in the town of Bethany happened just six days before Jesus's crucifixion. Some bible scholars believe that mixed with the blood, sweat, and exposed flesh of our Savior on that cross was still the lingering odor of that perfume. Now we must remember that this wasn't some sample spritz from Belk or Ulta; this was an entire jar of pungent, pure perfume that prepared the body of the Son of God for His death that saved us all. Even in the midst of great sacrifice, you could still smell the effects of her worship. To consolidate my point here, ponder this verse from Philippians 4:18 (HCSB) that talks of "a fragrant offering, an acceptable sacrifice, pleasing to God."

When was the last time you truly expressed your love for Jesus unashamedly?

A FINAL WORD
FROM KYLIE

First, I just want to say thank you from the bottom of my heart for taking the time to read through this devotional. I hope you were encouraged and empowered.

This project began in August of 2019 and was completed in December of 2021. I was seventeen years old at the start, and now here I am at nineteen. I'll be honest: I had my doubts that it would even get finished. There would be times when months went by, and I didn't write a word. It was discouraging, but I didn't want this to be forced. I wanted every word to be laid on my heart by God Himself. And I'm sure by now we're all aware that God has a timeline of His own, and His timeline ends up being so much better than mine.

Now let's be real: this book was difficult to write. I'm not a fan of being vulnerable and emotional, but God uses our vulnerabilities in powerful ways. My prayer for you going forward is that you say yes to God, no matter the cost, because you will be truly blessed for it. Now go. Be the next generation of powerful women for Christ. He is so proud of you, and so am I.

SCRIPTURES
REFERENCED

<u>Old Testament</u>

- Genesis 17 (NKJV)
- Genesis 32 (NKJV)
- Genesis 49:8–12 (NKJV)
- Exodus 34:4 (NKJV)
- Deuteronomy 3:22 (HCSB)
- Ruth 2:12 (NKJV)
- 1 Chronicles 29:9 (NKJV)
- Ezra 8:22–23 (NKJV)
- Nehemiah 9:17 (NKJV)
- Psalm 27:14 (NKJV)
- Psalm 45:11 (NKJV)
- Psalm 118:8–9 (NKJV)
- Psalm 142:3 (NKJV)
- Proverbs 13:20 (NKJV)
- Proverbs 16:9 (NKJV)
- Ecclesiastes 3:1 (NKJV)
- Micah 6:8 (NKJV)
- Zechariah 4:6 (NKJV)

New Testament

- Matthew 1:1–17 (HCSB)
- Matthew 2:11 (CSB)
- Matthew 7:7–8 (NKJV)
- Matthew 18:15 (NKJV)
- Mark 14:8 (HCSB)
- Luke 2:7 (CSB)
- Luke 5:1–11 (NKJV)
- Luke 15:31–32 (NKJV)
- Luke 19:5 (NKJV)
- John 6:35 (NKJV)
- John 11:3 (HCSB)
- John 12:1–8 (HCSB)
- John 21:15–17 (HCSB)
- Acts 9 (NKJV)
- Acts 17:27 (NLT)
- Romans 8:28 (NIV)
- Ephesians 4:29 (NKJV)
- Ephesians 4:31–32 (NKJV)
- Philippians 4:6–7 (NKJV)
- Philippians 4:18 (HCSB)
- 1 John 2:3–6 (NKJV)

LOVE LETTER
OUTLINE

1. Anger and Blame

I don't like it when _____

I resent _____

I hate it when _____

I'm fed up with _____

I'm tired of _____

I want _____

2. Hurt and Sadness

I feel sad when _____

I feel hurt because _____

I feel awful because _____

I feel disappointed because _____

I want _____

3. Fear and Insecurity

I feel afraid _____

I'm afraid that _____

I feel scared because _____

I want _____

4. Guilt and Responsibility

I'm sorry that _____

I'm sorry for _____

Please forgive me for _____

I didn't mean to _____

I wish _____

5. Love, Forgiveness, Understanding, and Desire

I love you because _____

I love when _____

Thank you for _____

I understand that _____

I forgive you for _____

I want _____

Printed in the United States
by Baker & Taylor Publisher Services